BOBBEE BEE

The HATER
(His Anger Teaches Everybody Reality)

Anti-Bullying Curriculum

Dr. Terrence Graham
MS,LCAS,DCC,CCSOTS,MAC,NCACII,SAP,CSAC(VA)

AuthorHouse™
1663 Liberty Drive
Bloomington, IN 47403
www.authorhouse.com
Phone: 833-262-8899

Because of the dynamic nature of the Internet, any web addresses or links contained in this book may have changed since publication and may no longer be valid. The views expressed in this work are solely those of the author and do not necessarily reflect the views of the publisher, and the publisher hereby disclaims any responsibility for them.

Any people depicted in stock imagery provided by Getty Images are models, and such images are being used for illustrative purposes only.
Certain stock imagery © Getty Images.

This book is printed on acid-free paper.

ISBN: 978-1-6655-2057-7 (sc)
ISBN: 978-1-6655-2058-4 (e)

Library of Congress Control Number: 2021905930

Print information available on the last page.

Published by AuthorHouse 04/08/2021

authorHOUSE®

Dedication

To my first born, William Shakur Graham, who took the mantle to being the face of BOBBEE BEE THE HATER and 5FT. PRODUCTIONS, LLC. I enjoy watching you grow into an intelligent young male who has super stardom at the top of the mountain you continue to climb.

To my second born, Xavier Tyrek Graham is the funniest and the most entertaining person in the family. I am very confident with your marketing skills and work ethic you will take 5FT. PRODUCTIONS, LLC places we can only dream of.

To my baby girl, Brianna L. Graham, the beautiful and the highly educated nurse of the family, as you grow older, I want you to fly out like a free bird and go forth and purse all your dreams.

To my mother, Queenia Elizabeth Graham, my number 1 FAN, thanks for providing me everything I needed to be mentally, physically, and spiritually competent to provide for family.

Contents

Acknowledgements

To my beautiful wife, Evelyn Graham, thanks for allowing me to be me and encouraging me to being the best version of myself.

To my brother, Eric D. Graham, the smartest man in the room, thanks for the criticism and pushing my buttons to be great. You are the most creative person I know and if you like something it must be damn good.

To my colleagues...THE SUPER FRIENDS.... Dr. Delton Devose, LPCS, LCAS, CCS, Leslie Hardy, MSW, LCSW, LCAS, Jamilah McClain, MSW, LCSW, Llewellyn Hicks, MSW, LCSW-A, James Turner, MSW, LCSW, and Monique Goodson, MS, LPC...the greatest therapists in the world. Thanks for believing in me, supervising and supporting me in every step of my career. I appreciate you... "The Super Friends."

Introduction

Bobbee Bee the **HATER** [His Anger Teaches Everybody Reality] is designed to meet the academic, developmental, and emotional and social needs of students K-12 and being able to answer the questions: Are you a bully?, Are you being bullied?, and What do you do if you are being bullied.

Bobbee Bee the **HATER** is a character created by Terrence Graham and Eric Graham.

Bobbee Bee the **HATER** is an obnoxious, opinionated 13 year old adolescent with a bad attitude from the city of brotherly love. His body language is bad and his grades are the worse in the state. He is totally misunderstood by his teachers and classmates. Ironically, he has been "bamboozled" and "brainwashed" by rap videos and enslaved by an endless supply of ESPN highlights. Bobbee Bee is the ultimate bully whose aspiration is to become only three things when he becomes an adult: [1] a rapper, [2] an athlete, and [3] a street hustler.

Bobbee Bee has been portrayed in three books entitled, "In the Mind of Bobbee Bee the Hater, Larry Long Legs featuring Bobbee Bee the Hater", A Sad Day for Jose Featuring Bobbee Bee the Hater, and a feature film entitled, "Bobbee Bee the Hater the Movie".

What is Bullying?

Bullying is unwanted verbal [teasing, and name calling], physical [hitting and punching], social, relational, and/or psychologically [exclusion, nonverbal, or emotional] aggressive behaviors among school children that involves **real** or **perceived** power imbalance.

The behavior is repeated or has the potential to be repeated over time.

It is essential to understand that the affects and stressors caused by being bullied can interfere with student's social development and learning in school. Children and youth who are bullied are more likely than other children to be depressed, socially isolated, anxious, have low self-esteem, and think about suicide. In contrast, children and youth who frequently bully their peers are more likely than others to exhibit the following behaviors: get into frequent fights, be injured in fights, vandalize or steal property, drink alcohol, smoke, be truant from school, drop out of school, and carry a weapon. Students who are bullied may fear going to school, using the bathroom alone, or riding the school bus.

Bullying peaks in middle school and starts to decline in high school. However, it never completely disappears. Boys tend to bully boys and girls. Girls tend to bully other girls.

Lesson 1: Initial Stages

Students Most Likely to Be Bullied

Some research suggests that students are most likely to be bullied because of perceived differences such as:

- Appearance of body size
- Perception of being gay, lesbian, bisexual, or transgender mannerisms
- Degree of masculinity or femininity
- Performance in school
- Race/ethnicity/national origin and/or religion
- Economic status
- A real or perceived disability
- A real or perceived mental/health concern

Possible Indicators of Students Who Bully

Research has indicated that the most prevalent indicators of students with the highest probability of bullying others are as follows:

- Larger or stronger than classmates
- Enjoy controlling others
- Lack of empathy for others
- Lack of compassions for others
- Feel more powerful than others
- Lack of emotion or remorse when discussing negative behaviors
- Enjoys conflict and refuses to accept responsibility for negative behaviors
- Often has behavioral, social, or academic problems at school

How Bullying Looks and Feels

In order to gain an understanding of how bullying looks and feels, we must first:

- Identify the problem
- Identify those kids involved with the problem ·
- Promote tolerance and teach conflict resolution
- Going to school without fear; teaching confidence building
- Provide access to mental health care
- Improve awareness and communication
- Develop peer support
- Enhance parent and community support

Lesson 2: Assessment

Are You a Bully?

The subsequent assessment will be utilized as a preliminary measure for help with determining if a student is demonstrating bullying behaviors.

		Yes	No
1.	Do you leave people out?		
2.	Do you ignore someone just to be mean?		
3.	Do you gossip about others?		
4.	Do you spread rumors?		
5.	Do you make fun of others?		
6.	Do you tell other who their friends can be?		
7.	Do you hit others?		
8.	Do you scratch others?		
9.	Do you punch others?		
10.	Do you spit on others?		
11.	Do you slap others?		
12.	Do you trip others?		
13.	Do you push others?		
14.	Do you kick others?		
15.	Do you throw things?		
16.	Do you damage other things?		
17.	Do you gang up on someone to hurt, scare or cause fear?		
18.	Do you take things that don't belong to you?		
19.	Do you tease or call names?		
20.	Do you use insults?		
21.	Do you use threatening words?		
22.	Do you intimidate?		
23.	Do you use any of the above behaviors through texting, Facebook, Twitter, or any other forms of social media?		

In questions, 1-6, if you choose **YES** in any of these questions, you are an **emotional** bully.

In questions, 7-18, if you choose **YES** in any of these questions, you are a **physical** bully.

In questions, 19-23, if you choose **YES** in any of these questions, you are a **verbal** bully.

Lesson 2: Assessment

Are You Being Bullied?

The subsequent assessment will be utilized as a preliminary measure for help with determining if a studen

		Yes	No
1.	Do you feel safe at school?		
2.	Has someone spread rumors or said mean things to you?		
3.	Do others tease you?		
4.	Has someone purposely embarrassed you in public?		
5.	Does a person often take something of yours and purposely break it?		
6.	Have you been left out of games, activities, or eating lunch with other people?		
7.	Have you been made fun of because of your clothes, hair, glasses, race, ethnicity, or religion?		
8.	Has someone threatened you over and over again?		
9.	Has someone repeatedly pushed, tripped, or hit you?		
10.	Have you been threatened or embarrassed through email, text, Facebook, or social media?		
11.	Do you stay away from school in order to avoid being teased, hit, or threatened?		

The HATER Method

HABIT - trying to replace the seven deadly habits with the seven caring habits which is the most critical aspect of improving relationships.

Seven Caring Habits	Seven Deadly Habits
Supporting	Criticizing
Encouraging	Blaming
Listening	Complaining
Accepting	Nagging
Trusting	Threatening
Respecting	Punishing
Negotiating Differences	Bribing or Control

ACTION- all actions are chosen often subconsciously in attempt to satisfy basic needs:

1. Love and belonging
2. Freedom
3. Power
4. Fun
5. Survival

THINKING- to control rational and irrational thinking of how the needs motivate your behavior.

EVALUATE - is what you are doing to get what you want...evaluate every action.

RELATIONSHIP- anyone who chooses to consciously create and use caring habits on place of harmful ones can satisfy their basic needs and build stronger relationships.

Lesson 3: Working Stages

Overview of Group Sessions

The groups are aimed to boost the self-esteem of teens who are bullied and the teens that are doing the bullying within the school environment using the principles and strategies of Reality Therapy.

The group will consist of eight [8] members each and will meet for about 45 to 60 minutes during school or after school for approximately 8 to 10 weeks.

Suggested Reading Materials for the Group Sessions

H.O.P.E. is Stronger than a Hurricane, Featuring Bobbee Bee the HATER

In the Mind of Bobbee Bee the HATER

Larry Long Legs, Featuring Bobbee Bee the HATER

Sad Day for Jose, Featuring Bobbee Bee the HATER

Pre-Group Activity: Feelings Checklist

Learning Reflection: It is okay to feel the way you feel, but it is as equally important to learn how to express how you are feeling on a given day in ways that does not cause pain.

Instructions: Before every group, the group members will complete a feelings check in. Please circle from the list of feeling words below to help you recognize and identify the feelings you are currently having.

Afraid	Frightened	Jealous	Proud
Aggressive	Frustrated	Joyful	Rejected
Alone	Glad	Left Out	Relaxed
Angry	Guilty	Lonely	Restless
Anxious	Happy	Loved	Sad
Bored	Hopeful	Miserable	Safe
Concerned	Hopeless	Miserable	Sorry
Confused	Hurt	Powerful	Tired
Depressed	Insecure	Powerless	Unloved

Session 1: Introduction and Formation

The group's initial session is for students to get to know each other and understand group rules. Group members are given the opportunity to discuss and develop roles which will help them to feel included in the group.

The teacher or counselor then introduces activities to get group members acquainted. He or she encourages participation and feelings belonging [self-expression] in a non-threatening atmosphere. Group members will begin to explore their feelings about being bullied in school.

Session 2 Activity: Personal HATER Chart

Based on Glasser's Choice Therapy, "a person-focused relationship based therapy everyone wants to be happy and the key to this is having satisfying relationships and making good choices".

The teacher/counselor facilitates building bonds and trust in the group through modeling. Students will learn the basics of the **HATER** method and begin to apply this into their school situations. The teacher/counselor then helps students understand that change comes from within themselves and explains the strategies to evoke positive change.

H = Habits

A = Actions

T = Thinking

E = Evaluate

R = Relationship

Group members will use their personal **HATER** chart to help develop goals for the next session. This will help them to review the **HATER** method and continue to evaluate their current actions in preparation for identifying new ways of doing things.

Session 2 Activity: Personal HATER Chart

Learning Reflection: you

Instructions:

What HABITS would You Change?

Habits	Barriers	%Completed	Delivery Date

What do you NEED for SURVIVAL?

Needs	Barriers	%Completed	Delivery Date

Who do you want to BUILD a RELATIONSHIP with?

Person	Barriers	%Completed	Delivery Date

Group Session 3: Building Self-Awareness and Self-Esteem

In this session the focus is on setting goals to enhance the student's self-esteem, help them to become more assertive, and be more connected to school community. The teacher/counselor helps students to create attainable goals for themselves to develop self- efficacy. Group members then share two goals they intend to strive for. Students will also identify and share with the group members 3 personal strengths. The facilitator (teacher/counselor) will lead discussions on the strengths they see in themselves and what others see.

Students will be encouraged to remind themselves of their strengths when they receive negative messages and especially when others try to bully them.

Session 3 Activity: How Do You Feel About Yourself?

Learning Reflection:

Instructions: In this activity, the group member will discuss the things they like about themselves and the things they would like to change about themselves.

1. Circle the physical traits you like about yourself.

   Hair   Face   Height   Weight   Build   Skin Color

2. Circle the personality traits you like about yourself

   Honest   Smart   Sociable   Funny   Athletic   Responsible
   Calm   Handsome   Pretty   Leader   Popular   Friendly

3. Name 3 traits that are important to you and explain why.

4. Name 3 things that you would change about yourself and explain why.

5. Complete these statement by using only positive words:
    - I am _____.
    - I will work on being _____.

6. Complete this statement
    o I want to stop thinking of myself as _____ and start thinking of myself as _____ .

Group Session 4: Practical Steps to Achieve Goals

During the middle session, counselor/teacher will help students develop practical steps for their plans. This will include activities to help students apply HATER to new strategies to deal with bullying in the school. For example, the facilitator could give a hypothetical example of a student who is bullied, and ask students to give possible suggestions that could help him or her gain control. Each group member will then look at his/her own experiences with bullying, and talk about practical steps that he or she can take to gain better control of their lives.

The counselor/teacher will continue to encourage and support students in order to further develop feelings of belonging in the group and at school and also to facilitate development of self- efficacy.

Session 4 Activity: Journaling Your Feelings

Learning Reflection:

Instructions: In this activity, the group members will write about what they can control at school/home/community.

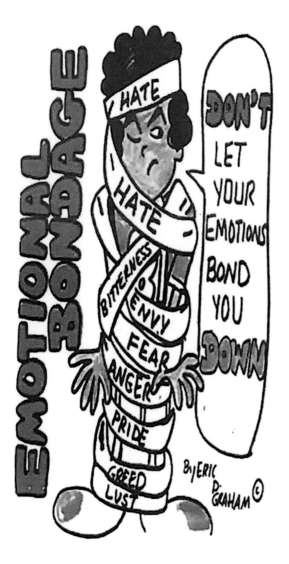

Session 5: Practicing Skills

In this session, group members will use HATER strategies learned in previous sessions, to evaluate how their assertiveness skills will help them achieve the goals of dealing with bullying. Activities could include recognition of the signals and their own responses to the signals (demonstrated through role plays).

Students could then talk about their successes or difficulties in trying to be more assertive. They can then rate their success on a scale of 1-10. The counselor could help group members adapt goals to meet individual needs, and affirm and praise their efforts at being assertive.

Session 6: Taking Responsibility
for Your Involvement

In this session, the facilitator will help group members use HATER to become more involved in the school community. The session will focus on the student's need for love and belonging. This will help group members to learn how to relate to others and develop partnership within the school. Then encourages each student to share what he or she considers to be his or her greatest contribution to the school/community.

Students will apply the HATER method to their need of being a part of their school community by listing their current attempts to get these needs met in pairs. Group members will identify what they are now doing, and try to identify strategies that are or are not successful. The counselor/teachers ends the session with a summary of the points agreed on in the session, and then introduces termination to students to get them used to the idea of moving on after the group experience.

Session 6 Activity: Picture Album

Instructions: The group members will develop a "picture album" by drawing themselves in the boxes below fulfilling their needs at school in various ways based on their ACTIONS.

BELONGING: develop
better relationships

POWER: need for
academic success

FREEDOM: need to
make choices

FUN: need to enjoy school

Session 7: Improving Communication Patterns

This session helps the group members become aware of the need for clear communications and how to communicate their needs accurately. They also will become aware of how "unclear" communication can cause conflicts.

The counselor/teacher could introduce an activity for students to role play a scenario where there is ineffective communication. Afterwards, the facilitator encourages them to talk about how the communication in the scenario could be improved. Another group of students will then role play effective communication based on pointers given. The facilitator can then help students to talk about how effective communication can help them to deal with bullying and also, help students to gain understanding that teachers and other members of the school are willing to help them.

As in all sessions, the counselor/teacher should model qualities such as warmth, acceptance, understanding to develop positive relationships in the group.

Session 7 Activity: How to Deal with the Bully

Learning Reflection: Take some time to reflect on how the project went for you. If you worked closely with a parent or another adult, think about how that went. Ask yourself the following questions and write your answers in your Main Lesson Book.

There is no simple way to deal with bullies when they strike. No BULLY is the same and what you may do in one situation may not work in another. Here are some tips below to help you communicate with the bully when he/she confronts you. Some of them may work with the BULLY in your school.

Instructions: Facilitator and group members should role play different situations in practicing these techniques.

1. Laugh along
2. Change the subject
3. Roll with the punches
4. Be assertive
5. Give the bully permission to tease you
6. Anticipate the bully's next moves/behaviors

Session 8: Moving Forward Bully Free!!!!!!!!

The final group sessions provides closure to the group experience. The closing activities should help members to continue the progress they have made in the group. Group members should feel a sense of accomplishment for all they have learned. They should be given the opportunities to express their thoughts and feelings about termination. Towards the end of the session, the facilitator hands out the evaluation sheets and makes the arrangements for follow-up.

References

Corey, G. (1995).**Theory and Practice of Group Counseling** (4th edition). Brooks/Cole Publishing Company, pg (41 0-413).

Graham, E.D. & Graham, T.W. (2005**). In The Mind of Bobbee Bee the Hater.** AuthorHouse Publishing.

Graham, E.D. & Graham, T.W. {2006). **Larry Long Legs featuring Bobbee Bee the Hater.** Author House Publishing.

Graham, E.D. & Graham, T.W. (2007). **A Sad Day for Jose featuring Bobbee Bee the Hater.** AuthorHouse Publishing.

Langan, P. {2003). **Bullying in Schools: What you need to know.** Townsend Press Book Center, pg (35-38).

Porter, R. (2011) .**Crafting a sales pitch for your grant proposal.** Research Management Review, Vol. 18, Issue (2) Fall/Winter 2011.

Printed in the United States
by Baker & Taylor Publisher Services